# WHAT
## DO YOU DO
## IN THAT
# ROOM?

Anthony J. Lapallo

What Do You Do In That Room?

Cover art and design by Sarah Lapallo with Inkwell Book Co.

Library of Congress Control Number: 2012955356

Lapallo, Anthony J.
What Do You Do In That Room?
First Edition

ISBN 0-9833982-9-1

PREFACE TO

## "WHAT DO YOU DO IN THAT ROOM?"

The poems in this book are by Anthony J. Lapallo, but
Anthony J. Lapallo does not exist.
Anthony J. Lapallo is a pseudonym for
Anthony J. Lapallo who does not exist.


This book exists because you are looking at it.
You exist because you are looking at the book.

The poems contained within will exist
if you bring them to life.
If you don't, don't blame the poet.
He doesn't exist.


## ACKNOWLEDGEMENT

This is to acknowledge the contribution of my Poetry Mechanic—
Mary Lou Lapallo

The Poetry Mechanic reviews my poetry:
She fixes it when it is broken.
She nurses it when it is sick.
She buries it when it is dead.

## Thank You

P.S. Like the poet, I don't exist either. Why should I take all the
blame?
—Mary Lou Lapallo


This is to also acknowledge my granddaughter, Sarah Amaris Lapallo,
also known as Amy, for her assistance in preparing the physical book.
She's sorry.

# TABLE OF CONTENTS

# WHAT DO YOU DO IN THAT ROOM?

A new style of poetry is floating around. Well, maybe not new. Depending upon whom you ask, it came from France in the nineteenth century, or farther back in time in Hebrew songs known as Psalms. I just caught up with it and in one of humanity's less classy traits, the world began when I noticed it. But you do not want to hear about my foibles, you rather get on with your own, so let me just say that the new style of poetry is called prose poetry. It is similar to free verse but on the page looks more like prose.

Prose has been with us for a long time. It is rather popular. We see it everyplace and even if we don't particularly recognize it as prose, it still plays its part in filling up blank newsprint and pages in books, and it gives otherwise blah pieces of paper something to say. Then there is its cousin, poetry. This has also been around a long time. We see it in birthday cards which say things like "Another year, oh dear; but have no fear, you can still shift in gear...Can't you?" We also see it in masterpieces which say things like "...happy...." (from "Ode on a Grecian Urn" by John Keats) or "I have heard...." (from Walt Whitman's "Song of Myself").

Now prose poetry is something that looks like prose but is really poetry because it plays tricks on the reader such as repeating certain words or sounds or characters. It also rhymes at times or reverberates with rhythm so as to certainly speak with throbbing strains to ears awaiting news. Stuff like that. It is also not rational like these words but speaks to the heart, to the soul. We all know that the heart and soul need sustenance, but sometimes we are so busy doing dying that we just don't have time to live.

Not everyone sees prose poetry as poetry. In the past, they placed this with free verse, which is writing lines of great variety and power, but without the comfort of regular rhythm and rhyme. They said that free verse was not poetry. That with free verse you got what you paid for. And if free verse was not poetry, neither was prose poetry which was simply prose. Times change and they do not say this about free verse anymore. Most poetry written today is vers libre, pardon my French.

However, many still have their doubts about prose poetry. I admit that it can be a trial at times to discern the difference between prose and poetry. Charles Dickens is known as a prose writer. "....and glass...." is a quote from one of his masterpieces, "The Old Curiosity Shop". But then we have a quote from the poet Emily Dickinson. In her poem "Glass was the Street" she says "Glass was..." So close is the prose to poem. If pure prose and pure poetry can be so similar, what can we say when prose and poetry, in the face of all that is logical, in the face of all that is rational, discard their "and" to enter the world of the unicorn, a world of solitary strength, a world of lonely power, until transformed by a pure maiden into a creature who sleeps; and who dreams.

In prose there are paragraphs, in poetry stanzas. Paragraph comes from a Latin word meaning beside and a Greek word meaning writing. Stanza is the Italian word for room. Just go into the room, turn on the light, look around, find a chair, and sit beside the writing. Then you can read, think, feel, or just take a word bath. So, no matter what you call it, the most important thing is what you do in that room.

Why did I say all that? Is this a book about prose poetry?

Let me answer the second question first. No. It is a book about poetry, my poetry specifically. And most of my poetry is not prose poetry.

But there are four reasons I said what I said. This was originally a part of the written materials that I handed out at a session on prose poetry that I conducted at my local senior center. I liked it so much that I didn't want to waste it, so I put it here at the beginning of my first book. The second reason is that I thought there was some good stuff here and I wanted you, my reader, to be able to read it. The third reason is that it sheds some light on why I titled the book the way that I did.

And the fourth reason I consider the most important so I gave it a paragraph all its own. Poetry, unlike prose, speaks to the undermind, the part of the mind that tells you what to say when someone asks you your name, or what to do next when you are driving a car or riding a bike or taking a walk. It seems to come out of nowhere. But it does not come from nowhere; it comes from a corner of your mind. When you read poetry, it goes to that corner and opens drawers from which come memories, feelings, dreams, hopes, wishes. But these things don't come rushing at you like the evening news on TV. They come gradually, they sneak up on you, and you need to be alert to them. But they won't come charging at you; you must search for them. The poet will not tell you what the poem is about, but he will give you clues as to its aboutness. In other words, the poet will give you a context in which to contemplate the poem.

My problem with many books of poetry is that I don't have a context for the poems and therefore I have difficulty is determining the poem's aboutness. In this book, I will give you a context to consider the poem's aboutness. Just keep in mind that this aboutness is not what each poem is about.

At this point, I think you will notice two things. One is that I like to talk to my reader. The other is that the paragraphs we both just finished are two darn long, so let's get on to the poetry.

# GOD FIRST

I am a Catholic, a Roman Catholic. I go to Mass, I say the Rosary, I try to live by the teachings of Jesus. But please do not call me a devout Catholic. I do not like that term. I prefer practicing Catholic. Like someone who plays music or baseball, I practice, trying to get better at it. Therefore, my Catholicism will influence my poetry, and because of this, I will start with my Catholic poems.

For those who are curious as to why I mentioned baseball above: I mentioned it because baseball is the official game of heaven.

## SEARCHING FOR CHRISTMAS

I went to a house where there
was no house, knocking on a door
which was, as I looked, nowhere

to be found, but it opened more
or less, and standing in front
of me on a bottomless floor

was an old man who bore the brunt
of everything, or so it seemed.
Brunt isn't right, maybe rumpled

is a better word in a cleaned
sort of way, like a grandfather,
or no cup, just coffee with cream.

He didn't speak but rather
gave me a choice of a chair
or another chair, no matter.

Not speaking, he said the pair
was there at the moment, a light
over his head and his son in air.

Again not speaking he said right
now what can I do for you,
and I said that before night

fell, I wanted to find Christmas.
This thirst was old and new;
then wine was in my glass.

From searching a hunger grew,
which he also saw and said,
"I made a bread, just for you."

I went to a house where there
was no house,
knocking on a door which was,
as I looked,
nowhere

I was there

## THE FISH

two groups of people should not read this poem:
these are catholics and non-catholics;
consider yourself warned by the metronome
ticking with a silent measuring yardstick,
keeping some things in an irregular way
regular. quietly becoming awestricken.


I am a follower of Jesus
who feels typecast in saying His name.

Many scorn or smirk or look away. If they speak,
       "not scientific"
                they say.

But solemn faces with Bibles and dispatches from on-high,
      Although I need the living water,
             they leave me dry.

"Come follow Me" is what He said, and He went through life
      and He went through dead,
           and back to life, just as He said.

The scorners smirkers are not scientific workers who observe
  and count.
      If they were they would not discount
           the ineffable.

The solemn faces are loquacious and tenacious as they preach
  and pray.
      But do they really say that Jesus the Christ actually walked
           on the ground when He came this way?

 So let us ask: Did Jesus walk the earth and
die, then rise from the dead as many say?
Or is this just a lie, told to help us past those
thoughts of our own dark night of decay?

I say "Yes He rose" and I work with grace
and take the scripture and my interiority
and tradition and the world of the spy
and of my position see the feasibility.


Why the spy?

The spy having his tradecraft and position in the minority,
The spy searching around with his eye,
The spy loooking for what should not be there,
The spy loking for what is missing, doing the work of the spy.

When I spy I see after the resurrection Jesus appearing
to people suddenly and just as mysteriously disappearing.
    Jesus going through walls to meet the apostles.
    Jesus greeting them.
    Jesus speaking with them.
    Jesus giving them cheer.
    Jesus breaking bread.
    Jesus giving them to eat.
    Jesus eating a fish.


You wonder what this is about, let us be clear.
The end of this story is coming near.
You can make up a story to any drumbeat.
But the right one is that which makes the story complete.

Like a good spy, note what is there, not a wish.
When Jesus left, He left with a shwish;
But at the same time, unnoticed, so did the fish.

# THE OLD PRIEST

The fall chill lingers in the old church
while early dawn darkness fades
from stained glass visions of
saints in obsolete clothing.

A bell tinkles to announce the arrival
of the old priest and his young acolyte
going unto the altar, the joy of the old
man's youth, the youth merely young.

With deliberate steps, the old priest
climbs the mountain where Moses
encountered God, and begins in the
name of the Trinity, all one by one.

The old priest washes the world's dust
from the garment of his soul, repeats
the lessons that are repeated again and
again until they become new, and then,

in the name of the congregation, about
eleven, no wait! here comes a few more,
offers their gifts – their bread, their wine,
their hearts – all one by one.

And like on the mountain where the bush
burns but is not consumed, bread and wine
change but are not assumed by the eye to be
what the soul knows is resumed.

And then the old priest feeds the congregation,
that group of miscellaneous folk who left
the chill that is now fading for the warmth
of the fire that burns but does not consume.

The old priest, in the best tradition, cleans
and puts away, and sends the folks out to life,
to what is now the coming of the light
and the beginning of a new day.

The old priest comes down from the mountain
and exchanges his obsolete clothes for the
garments of now, and silently prays that
the young acolyte won't always be young.

# REVELATION TO A DEAD PAINTER

I painted many things:
landscapes, seascapes, forests with
maple trees by roads and rocks;
mothers, children, workmen, and even
that great staple, my dreams.

I used watercolors and oil paint:
on canvas, on wood, on paper;
drawings with charcoal, with pencils;
collages with scissors and paper and glue;
and no one had a complaint.

But all my life, I wanted to paint God.

I made appointments, but He broke them.
I went into the wilderness, but He left
before I arrived; I went out into the deep
and He was gone, leaving only fish.
I went into the multitudes alone.

God would not stay still.
He went hither and yon.
He went up and down.
If I was here, He was there.
God would not stay still.

While sustaining the search, I died.
Finally, at last, I would get to paint God.
However, in heaven
I did a lot of jumping around,
going here and there, up and down.

You see, it was me who would not stay quiet.

God was the One Who was Still

ESCHATOLOGY

The
story
of man through
time reveals what
happened to me when
I entered time since there
was no where else I could go.
I swam a while in a pleasant
pool, then took the plunge into the big
wide world.  Time is quick.  Here comes time for school.

In a flash a mate, a child, and a place
in the sea's churning, swirling whirlpool.
Soon the waters settle and life
cruises toward the western port.
I'm still here, with the cod,
but checking my mail
daily since I
expect a
note from
God.

## MIRACLES

Seated in my easy chair near the fireplace,
I read from a book of essays by C.S. Lewis,
a man who wrote stories for children
and ideas for grownups. He spoke of miracles.

Like a seed planted in soil, under the sun,
with water added, growing into a small plant,
getting more water and sunlight and time and then
it shows the fruit. Amazing how that happens.

And along comes a human with his brain,
gray and white glop, wet, that water again,
taking the fruit, figuring how to ferment,
and then the wine, an amazing miracle.

And then he told of Jesus, a guest at a wedding,
in Cana, a place like here, seeing that the hosts
have run out of wine, the party is still going on,
or at least they would like it to.

The Chief Steward told Mary, Jesus's mother,
about their plight. Mary told Jesus and he said
"So?" Mary told the Steward to do what he asked,
and then she looked at her son and said

"Go." And being the good son he asked for jugs,
large jugs, and said "Fill them with water."
Now we have water and we have light and
we have time, and then, now we have wine.

C.S. Lewis, speaking to me from his pen
writing long ago, told me that what happened
to that seed planted in the soil and thought about
by a brain, was the same as what was

when Jesus looked at those jugs of water
and produced the same result, wine; miracles?,
yes, both times, it's just that Jesus works faster.
But wait, Jesus has made more than mere wine.

The bride and groom were his friends,
their family were friends, and their guests
were friends. Jesus said "I call you friends
and give you not a miracle, but a Gift."

That gift, the wine, would surely be drunk
that day if not the next.
Today, all the guests are gone.
And the bride and groom are no longer with us.

But the story is still here.
And it comes to us over the ages.
More than a miracle.

A Gift

# PURGATORY

Theologically, people don't like purgatory.

World Series        Super Bowl        Olympic Gold

Just award the trophy

No workout                No daily grind
No pushing yourself       No testing the soul

Just give the prize and let everyone clap.

Ah—sweet unreality.

And then there is cancer.
An ache here, a pain there, with
total devastation leading to
the incarnation of the cancer wars.

Eventually the dust settles revealing
casualties and survivors.
Theologically, people don't like purgatory.
In the distance a robin sings.

# TO A COLD DAY IN HELL

What if it really happened?

Temperature

plunging

down

down

until it was so cold that Hell Froze Over

Would someone call a plumber or a priest?
If  a plumber, where would he find the controls, the wiring,
the main unit?....do such things exist in a non-solid world?

If a priest, what would he know about plumbing,
if indeed this is a plumbing problem?

What about the inhabitants?  How would they react?
Would they cheer and say "Yea! No more fire!"
Or "I can't believe it's this cold.  This is why I left Cleveland"?

Would stores suddenly spring up, selling sweaters and warm socks?
If so, who would run them?  Where would they get stock?

And then there is the devil and his minions.
It won't be long and they will
be out of a job.

Do you think that maybe, just maybe (don't get excited;
notice I say maybe)

A group of Angels might just be sent
to open a travel bureau?

# THE GROCERY BUSINESS

One morning I was working in the Eden Garden Grocery
when this snake walked in and asked to see the fruit stand.
I pointed and he looked at the pears and peaches, grapes
and plums, oranges and lemons, and of course, the limes.

His face furrowed into a frown as if it were plowed and then
he asked, shyly, what kind of fruit would impress a lady.
That's hard to say I said, since I heard of a lady, but
had never seen her or anyone like one anywhere in these parts.

He explained that she had a man for a companion and they were
often together, walking and frolicking in the Garden in the warm
light of day and even in the soft nights that followed. He wanted
something that she and her man could partake of together.

I hadn't seen a man either, but I explained that the Grocery
was not actually in the Garden but just outside its borders.
However, a lot of fruit was shipped from there to here
and it filled the produce aisle with a heavenly glow.

I heard the Garden was a beautiful place, and I was planning
to go there for summer vacation next year. However,
I had never been there, up to now content to stock the shelves
with its bounty and wait for the customers to come in.

The fly boys came in regularly and purchased the fruit. Regular
customers they were, crossing the border every sixth day to get
a supply to enjoy on their day off. They never paid but no matter.
I took care of them and then had all I needed, always.

The snake asked if I ever had apples. I said I heard of them
but so far they never came in my regular deliveries. Maybe
they were still under development. Then he asked about the
smart fruit from the Knowledge Tree. Do I ever get that?

I said I heard of it but it didn't come here. Something about
it being dangerous in the wrong hands. Too difficult for
most folks to handle. Too many parts. Too complex.
The snake smiled a slight sneer and then left. Too bad....

## JESUS CHRIST SUPERSTAR

is a rock musical

from the mind of Tim Rice and Andrew Lloyd Webber
based upon a true story conceived by an inconceivable mind.

The title role in this drama was for forty years lived by a man
named Ted Neeley, on stage and screen and in audience hearts.

That is a long time to be playing a role, but I have been playing
me for as long as I remember, sixty plus many elongated years.

My story is true but not on view on stage or screen, but on streets,
in rooms, on buses, on trains, in parks, in sun, in rain and I hope,

in some hearts. My story was originally conceived by Mom and Dad,
reworked by them, and polished by others in the worldly scene.

No getting around it though, Ted Neeley played Jesus while I only
played me, so of the first meeting in heaven, his is the one to see,

with the Father looking on while the Spirit covers from above, and
the Son, seated comfortably, smiling on all creation, radiates his love.

Mr. Neeley awaits his turn, with me standing next in line, then in awe
and wonder, makes his way to the Holy Place after receiving a sign.

Jesus sees Ted and says with a glow

"I know who you are. You played me on earth.
I also once appeared in that same tableau.
That is why you are here now
in this place of peace and mirth."

"And you. Next in line. You have good seats. Enjoy the Show."

# HOLY SATURDAY

This is the day
that follows the day
called Good,
and waits for....

In the field, mist caresses the gray stone while guards
watch.  Except for quiet and cold, they are alone
murmuring to each other of the shards of
the past day, past understanding, thankfully past.

That was bad.  They are all bad.  But this defied
comprehension somehow, as if heaven wept;
and if heaven cried, what of us under its tears?
What will come of us, by the stone's step?

What will come of us, by the stone, in mist,
waiting for....

....morning

# FIRST COMMUNION

Sunday at the local Catholic Church
is First Communion time again,
although the interesting thing
about First Communion
is, every time is....

In a melding act of love        two enter        and become one,

The new one is one with water        until their unity overflows
                            to become one with air.

And the milk of human and human kindness unites two into one,
        until human fades
            and
                kindness
                    remains,

    creating longing that we may be whole        again,

        creating longing that we may be whole        always.

Then comes the time when there is the Bread and the Wine,
        and then the time when there is First Communion,
            and then the time after First Communion.

The new time, the time after, unites with the time before,
                    in the time now.

    And the wine of Divine and the bread of Life unite
                in a melding act of Love,

where one becomes whole again        where one becomes whole always

    because, and this is the interesting thing, every time is....

                            ....always First Communion

# PROZENPOME

You might have noticed that the last two poems had a somewhat different form. These are in a form I invented called a Prozenpome. This section will tell you all about the Prozenpome.

I invented the prozenpome to make it easier for readers to become part of what they read. A prozenpome is a writing that begins like prose, transforms quickly into poetry, and ends as....

Wonder why the ellipses.

Prose is writing that explains, that appeals to our rational mind's need to understand the world and our place in it. It explains what is outside of us, even if it is inside like our heart and our lungs.

But we have more than one inside. In addition to what the surgeon sees, there is another inner world seen by the spirit. That is the one that the poet writes about.

We usually understand prose quickly unless it refers to a field of which we have little or no knowledge, or uses the specialized language or history of that field. Examples would be science, religion, mythology, art, sports, etc.

Poetry can be more difficult because it is referring to internal states or thoughts or feelings for which we do not have good descriptive words. As a result, poetry takes more time than prose to read and understand. Think of it like this. Novels are about 300 pages long and we read them once. A poem may be one page long but we have to read it 300 times to fully comprehend it.

This said, poets, if they want their readers to comprehend what they write, must give them some scaffold or organizing principle upon which to construct a meaning. Otherwise, the poem, no matter how good, only becomes a miscellaneous collection of words.

The prozenpome is designed to give this structure to the reader. It begins with a title stating what the poem is about, followed by what is essentially a short prose-like statement making the topic clear, but leaving a space to wonder. Then there are stanzas or other constructions written as poetry to get inside the situation referred to in the title and introduction. There is no rule as to form, type of stanzas if any, number of lines in a stanza or feet in a line, or rhyme scheme. This is left up to the poet.

The stanzas are followed by a single line or a line and a part of another line, or maybe a few more lines or some other construction less than a full stanza....

Wonder why the ellipses.

And then these two wonders come together to form....

Well, you know. After all. It is poetry.

# WEDDING NIGHT

The newly married couple
on their wedding night
go to bed and....

The sun's light glitters on the fecund earth
which heaves and falls in a chaotic dance.
They beguine and bourree in watered mirth,
then sit and sing to this ever new chance.

The light goes short as the shadows grow long,
while birds return to their roosts.  Flowers fold
their petals to close, humming a silent
song.  The night uncloaks its chronicle old

as the earth and sky join to come one, and....

.....sleep

## A POETRY READING

Sitting alone with a crowd
intimate only with our chairs
poets propelling words
we grasp at,
while we hope
to....

The back of the teeth           ticking off the d's and t's

      followed by o's and ah's     the drone of m's and n's numbing

   taking us directly to an under    where we   stand    not know   ing

           what has been said.

Our head snaps, eyes pop awake        the others in the room

    silent         still      sure of themselves      it seems

they know    have heard    what I have not   so I listen more intently

and catch a word    and the word is    "simply"   which can mean

soley or barely or merely or purely or only while the five fingers point
in as many directions as five fingers can point     and then
          the moderator     stands and says

       "Thank you for coming. I hope
       our time here was productive.
       Have a pleasant evening
       and Good night."

The others stand, I stand, we put on our coats, we walk out the door.
They seem so smiley while I feel so simply in all its possible meanings
thinking tonight I can only hope to....

                  ....dream.

## SPAGHETTI

Nobody eats spaghetti,
nowhere notime never.
They say they do but
never trust they. They
cover up. They really
eat....

      red
    flame and hot
passion fire on a plate

                                          black
                                   octopus ink
                              direct from Sicily

                tomato
            garlic and spice
         basil is good, very good

    white
  flour with milk
with chicken bullion

                                  then blend
                              leeks and salt
                        some pepper, not much

                or butter
                   with
            lemon and lobster
              or clam

Anything to keep us from eating spaghetti.
Spaghetti is only an excuse to eat....

                                      ...sauce

# FOOD POEMS

The last prozenpome leads us naturally into the food poems.

We will start with Doors since most of us get our food from the grocery store.

And then Coupons which help us get our food.

And then the food itself. I especially like Bananas since this poem solves one of the great problems in poetry: finding something to rhyme with orange.

Bon Appetite

DOORS

In-door

| | | |
|---|---|---|
| fruit | vegtable | aisle |
| berries | beet | leeks |
| spaghetti | noodles | soup |
| sugar | teas | coffee |
| beans | can | corn |
| muffins | fudge | bread |
| cookie | chips | grain |
| soap | towels | dry goods |
| fish | meat | milk |
| money | bag | change |

Out-door


COUPONS

By buying two you get a dollar off.
But buying one you pay full price.
And buying nothing you keep it all.

Buying nothing enough times gives you lots
of nothing. And also a good tax rate.
No maintenance charges either. Pure profit

which you will carefully invest in more
coupons. Do not see where you can lose here.
But you have to watch the expiration date.

## ORANGE SODA

Frank O'Hara is a great American Poet.
I'm not.

Frank O'Hara wrote poems on his lunch hour.
I don't.

Frank O'Hara saw the limits of human life.
I'm not there yet.

Frank O'Hara liked music and art.
I can't sing or draw.

Frank O'Hara wrote of dirt and sex, but not
necessarily in that order or context.
I'm not saying anything.

Frank O'Hara put orange in a poem, even
when it didn't belong.

                    Finally, I'm vindicated.  At lunch
                    I have a real orange soda.

## MAKING CHICKEN SOUP

In the beginning is the stove
and then the pot.  Turn
on the fire and make it hot.

Then spin your can round
the opener square, and
put it in the pot          overthere.

Oops!  Forgot the prime thing in the loop.
Must read the label          It needs to say
chicken soup.


## TOMATO SAUCE

The thinker thinks and the walker walks
while the runner runs toward Tuesday.
As for me, I grip my pen and guide it
across the page where I send ink into its fibers.

All this is done in the surrounding air
of a world gone global, said as if it once
was a rectangle which lost all of its angles
in the heat of the walking running.....

Let's take a moment and put it at the end
of the previous line—Now that that's done
it's Thursday and where, you ask,
as promised above, is the tomato sauce?

To be honest, I don't like tomato sauce.
But you can find it cooking
in my wife's poem.

## FISHING

In the grocery store there are fish,
fish waiting for us to bite.

We circle around, calculating weight,
looking at the sleek beauty,

lured by allures, fingering our coin
like round worms of steel and

then we strike....caught!

Then, in ignorant bliss we go
to our basket of a house,

unaware that our spicing and
dressing and cooking are our

undoing as we, believing in
our invincible eating,

become the fish.

# BANANAS

Bananas, bananas, every store has bananas.
If you don't have bananas, the customers go bananas.

Why bananas you say?  Well, they are easy to cook.
Put your stove on no-heat and peel and play.

Bananas are good for you too.  They build strong bones
and teeth and if not, so what?  You don't have to chew.

At night when the light goes away, you recall
the bananas' bright yellow, how it cheered the day.

Then you lie on your bed when eyes heavy seem,
slip into sleep, and dream the banana-inspired dream

    where banana rhymes with orange

## PORK RIBS, BONELESS

I see them first in the supermarket
among the chops, ribs, and roasts.
I see them next as they head north
into the icy realms of my freezer.
I see them later in barbeque sauce in a
pan before the stove's sunlike heat.

Before something can be gone, must it exist?
Before there is less of something, must we
have more or at least some?

Can less add to something and make it more?
Can more be the death of some, so we
are blinded to the these?

And these, yes, thou art not these art thou?
Unless thou art them, but who is thou without
something else there.

Always something and now there is there,
right where you always find it,
under your nose, or maybe foot.

Now you see them on the round white plate.
Please don't ask me what they mean.

# EATING WATERMELON

It was summer in the grocery aisle so there was
   watermelon.
I was wet with sweat, my throat was dry, I hungered
   for sweetness.
I had money and then I didn't, but now the watermelon
   was mine.
My watermelon and I went home.

I first feasted my eyes on the watermelon, green and red,
   the green
Giving permission to enter, the red saying stop and look
   when you do.
And I saw the red, wet fruit; not a red of fire but of quiet
   passion,
Like peace.

Eating a watermelon is like heaven with its sweet, wet
   consolation.
The first bite is best as hunger and thirst welcome melon's
   response.
The invitation continues and we revel in our new found
   fortune, but
Something shifts.

As I go further into the watermelon, the flavor slowly
   fades.
The color is lighter too, as if the melon is slipping from
   my grasp.
And what was once succor is now like sin as bitterness
   signals
A belly-ache.

I sat alone as night fell and in the dark and quiet I waited
   for relief.
In the silence, someone came and told me of another
   grocery aisle
Where all take of the same watermelon and all eat always
   only the first bite.
This is good for me to know.

## A THEME IN MUSIC IS LIKE
## WATERMELON IN A POEM

A hot, thirsty man wants watermelon.
So the poem places the man where
  watermelons are
And the man makes a melon his own
  and takes it home.

There the hot, thirsty man meets the melon.
The poem describes the cool, wet wonder
  of the melon
And the personal pleasure procured from
  the melon's bounty.

But poems want drama and it will be theirs.
The man travels far beyond the borders
  of wisdom
And pillages the watermelon without regard
  to the return.

The melon seeks its revenge and takes it.
Poems want justice and this one balances
  the books
As the man suffers the fate of the glutton,
  the belly-ache.

This poem, however, is a good poem.
It wants the return to wisdom, not the man's
  demise.
And after suffering, sagacious suppositions
  save our man.

So, when you hear music
listen for the watermelons.
Stay with the melons
through all the notes.
But take care to stay
within the notes.

Songs have no mercy

RED-HAIRED LADY
IN BED
UNDER WHITE SHEET
RIGHT HAND AT END
OF BARE SHOULDER AND ARM
HOLDING BLACK PHONE


```
BEDBEDBEDBEBEDDBEDBEDBEDBEDBEDBEDBEDBED
BED                                   BED
BED        RED HAIR                   BED
BED                                   BED
BED            RIGHT HAND  HOLDING     BED
BED              BLACK PHONE          BED
BED                                   BED
BED                        ELBOW      BED
BED                ARM                BED
BED                                   BED
BED          BARE SHOULDER            BED
BED                                   BED
BED WHITESHEETWHITESHEETWHIESHEETWHITESHEE
BED    WHITESHEETWHITESHEETWHITESHEETWHITES
BED        WHITESHEETWHITESHEETWHITESHEETBED
```

            if this looks excessive
            i have to say it is

            if this raises eyebrows
            i have to say it does

            there must be a better way
            to buzz     the pizza man


            also, the poem is
            somewhat disheveled, but
            don't cry out for a ban    red-heads have to eat too

## NOTE TO READER:

You might have noticed by now that some of my poems
Are serious reflections on truth: truth is good.

Of my other poems, many go from sublime to
Ridiculous. Ridiculous can be playful,
Or silly but that is the chance you take in play.
You decide which is which. Then you have it your way.

But don't be too quick to judge. Take "Pork Ribs, Boneless".
What seems like mindless meandering could, if you take a
Second look, be like Jazz. The theme is stated in the first stanza
And repeated in the last.  In between are all sorts of improvizations
For the entertainment of the poet and, hopefully, for the reader.
Look at some of the other poems and zee if you zee anything else.

OK pardner, let's do some **NATURE POEMS** like real poets do.

## FLOWERS

Who looks
at the flowers in spring or summer,
or even fall.

Who sees
as they smile in silence or quietly
call

to us who are eating or thinking,
but not noticing at all
their color and their silent call.

Who thinks
of beauty in those who live among us now,
or even then.

Who wonders
about their words and thoughts and
faces

while we are planning or deciding,
but not noticing at all
their words and their silent call.

Who is touched
at the simple joy of their fragrance
or their bulbous funny nose.


Not I.

Here in winter.
In the land of ice and snow and cold.
In bitterness and death.

Too late.

I remember.

SNOW FALLS

Snow falls.
White on green or gray or brown.
White in air or hill and town.

Snow falls.
Cold and wet and chill.
Coating trees and roads and hill.

Snow falls.
Slippery on paths and streets.
Sliding into unlikely meets.

Snow falls.
Quietly in soft but winter air.
Quickly in windy puffs along the stair.

Snow falls.
Shivering am I
Standing high.

Snow falls.
But down below
Buried warm and dry.

Snow falls.
Where would you rather be?
Warm and dead or here with me?

## TWO TREES

evergreens, one in front of the other,
one of them, the one in front, gnarled,
grotesque, tortured, branch and bark cut away
so only barkless sawed-off limbs remain.

If death were photographed this is the image.
It must be above ground only because
death is also above ground as below,
and this gnarled, grotesque tree is death.

The back tree overshadows the death tree,
looming over it with three stalks of green,
forming a trinity of an embrace
with a rich ineffable color.

Life looms over the world in face of dross.
The green tree overcomes the tree of loss.

THE HOWLING NORTH WIND
FRIGID FINGERS AT THE THROAT
ICY CICLES DOWN THE CHEST
PAIN, NATURE'S WHOLE NOTE
                and
MY FAVORITE APPLIANCE


Breeze does blow winter;
Freeze you faint heart;
Wheeze icy breath and
Ease will depart.

Feet fly to home,
Entreat at the door;
Street leave behind,
Greet the stove once more.




As long as it is winter, let's go skiing.

And if we are going skiing, let's go big time:

Let's go skiing in the ALPS

## SKIING IN THE ALPS

The rite de passage from the lodge.


softly, the white sitting, softly,
waiting to greet the one, who
shuffling with long clumsy feet,
shuffling to the seat, which also
waits for the journey, is wary.

the mountain going higher than up
can go, and you are up with more
up to go but not for you, for now
you stop and see the down that
waits for you, far below.

it is cold but not the cold of shivers
but of hurt, the cold that is not cold
but hurt and pain; quick put on
the mask, the face guard, so as
not to hurt, not to burn but to spurn

the lift, with feet up and then down
off the seat moving away from followers
who need your space as others will need
theirs, go to the right or the left or ahead,
resetting hat, goggles, scarf, adjust poles

to be ready for the journey that is so
there in front of you with so much
behind you and so far to go, too far,
why, why am i here, and now
it's time, time to push off and go

down, going, down, going down,
snow flashing, going, flashing
snow, wind blowing, blowing,
thinking turn, turn, turn again with
stinging, stinging snow and wind


and then only a blur, the blowing blur
which is nothing but blur and then
no eyes but sight and no ears but sound
and no smell but smell and no touch but touch
and then the stop. and then premature.


The taste of the lodge.


About now, I'm ready to relax and have some warmer weather.

What's a more relaxing place than a Babbling Brook?

# THE BABBLING BROOK

The babbling brook babbles —— always.
After too much, like, say snow,
it is quiet for a while, but snow's
   effects do not stay.

The babbling brook winds
here and there as if it had
   no destination.
Where anywhere is just fine.

The babbling brook tumbles on over rocks,
whispers sweet nothings to the shore.
If fish swim on by it waves them through,
with everyone smiling, no one is stressed.

The babbling brook is a friend of trees,
although the brook does the talking
and the trees just stand there, listening,
like a confessor from the archdiocese.

You say for my thoughts a penny,
how do I know of these natural facts?
Easy I say. Of all that I said, it is
all about my cousin Benny.

## BLOWING LEAVES

When a leaf blows down the road
and the poet grabs a pen,
one thinks of a nature song.

One that extols the wild's ways
with wind, a road, and a leaf.
Yes, but with a different flow.

The leaf continues moving
and the wind persistently blows
while the road remains the stage.

But the bard's curtains are drawn,
while gas, water, light engage,
as the poet's bills come due.

## A PARK BENCH


A park bench, usually in a park;
it could be along a path,
or in your place
in the back yard

                          pure potential


And then someone sits in it;
nobody notices the bench,
not those sitting
not those passing

                          looking or not looking


At this point it should be actual;
but it is like a vision of God,
clearly there and
clearly invisible

                          knowing and not knowing


A park bench is not self-conscious;
no matter where it is,
it just is
just there


                          being not doing


And being can be done anywhere;
in a park or in a path or in a yard,
by anything
anywhere

## START WITH YESTERDAY

An eight-year old boy short for his age
walks among tomato plants tied to sticks;
the plants, unlike the boy, are skyward,
mouth-watering red fruit hanging down.

Just beyond the boy's backyard—the woods,
and berry picking beckoning with blue
and red and black, fruit again, the wild side,
the thrill of filling the basket among thorns.

And the flowers.  If eyes could eat, these
would be their berries, their tomatoes;
but the soul has vision and swallows them
into an inner joy of yellow, red, and green.

A sixty-three year old man looking out
over fifty-five years sees those same
tomatoes, same berries, same flowers:
God and the Farmer's Market are timeless.

## POETRY POEMS

All poets, or maybe just some poets, or maybe just modern poets, or maybe some modern poets, or maybe I overstated this whole thing; but there are poets, really, who like to write poems about poetry.

And when they write these poems, they are telling their readers to stop running from poetry. Instead, embrace poetry. There really is something in it for everyone. Everyone has hopes, dreams, even fears. Everyone wants consolation, joy, laughter, freedom from fear, and peace.

And when you are consoled, where are you consoled?

And when you have joy, where does it reside?

And when you laugh, from where does it come?

And when you are free from fear, where are you exactly?

Is it the place where peace is?

And that is where poetry goes, inside you, the place where you really live.

Now people often ask of poems "What do you mean?"
That is the worst question you could possibly ask.
Do you ask of a meal, what do you mean?
Do you ask of sleep, what do you mean?
Do you ask of the rain, what do you mean?
Do you ask of the shining sun, what do you mean?
Do you ask of a loved one, what do you mean?

Instead, don't ask a poem anything.
Just invite it inside,
    to the place where you really live,
    and be with it for a while.

OK. Let's get the bad stuff out of the way first.

# BAD POEM

(i paean omnis non-dog-lovers ubique

—Dog)

These words from a litter of syllables
chew tables, chairs, and pillows
and make these thoughts unintelligible.
Bad Poem

They whine when I dine, breaking flows
of the wise ponderings of the sage,
shamelessly drooling where anything goes.
Bad Poem

This is a bad poem messing up the page
with stale words from yesterday,
like a hopeless play on a barren stage.
Bad Poem

Like Lady Macbeth's dog, go out I say,
out damned Spot, and do not return,
do not trouble my musings again today.
Bad Poem

Once outside, it never does learn
and chases the cat-like phrases
which claw its meanings to a burn.
Bad Poem

So off to the poem vet in town spaces
we go, to treat the torn meters,
sore rhymes, metaphor's remaining traces.
Bad Poem

What the poem vet says does not make sense.
I need to go now and get a license.
For Bad Poem?

## BAD POET

Life is serious and
I am being frivolous.

Poets write of their travails,
While I suffer silently

Without a pen in my hand.
Then I am moved to write

About God—peeking
At us, smiling.

And then chiming like
a drunk passing a bar,
I unthinkingly
begin rhyming.

## BARGAIN BASEMENT POETRY

I read in a book somewhere
that some poets take months
to write a poem, while others
do half a hundred drafts.

I don't work that way.
Instead, I take a stroll down
one of my mind's streets
where the word guy
has his shop.

I go in and  wander around
looking at this one then that,
this goes good with slogans,
that one with clipped contractions,
and these are those that tell
of alliteration.

I then make my selections
and put them in a sack
which I take back to my
computing machine
(no quill pens for me; they break down)
to put in some kind of order.

Then I assemble this wordage
into lines, some long, some not,
until I run out of words
or ideas, but that is another story.

So?  Is this poetry?
What are my words worth?
Compared to him, not much,
but think of this:
At this moment, I'm all you've got.

# BOMBERS

I'm a secret agent
so      you        can't
see
                    my face


                                        or you can't
    know                      my
        name


But I can give you an idea of how it works.

The intelligence
                    crosses our desks
                                in the form of


                a poem

The first thing we do is notice what we see when we look around.
We try to grasp the essence, the gist, the what's it all about
impressions before its meaning goes to ground and be-
comes ineffable.

Then looking out the corners of our eyes
We try to find the ineluctable before
                                        it is covered in od wrds
                making it elegantly inelastic and o pay ic

In other words, what is peculiar or eccentrically curious.


Then we search for the code.
The code can be tricky:
    unusual words,,,
    usual words    used unusually,,  or just
    usual words

Sometimes they evoke pictures or feelings,
but we are not fooled because they are
not real:
        they are part of the code.

Then we examine the words more closely
wondering why this one instead of that one, or
does up mean down or down over or
upper lower or lower lower still.

Through patience and persistence
we crack the code and see
the meaning.


Then we contact the air force
who send in the bombers
and blow it all up.

DANCERS


Poets make theaters on paper stages.
They place scenery on these stages.
Things like mountains or streams
or cities or even space-age
accoutrements are placed there.

Poets then place actors in theaters
and let them tell a story, or not.
Sometimes they just let them be
or don't place them there at all.
Sometimes no one is there.

Readers open their books and go
to these theaters, going with hope
and anticipation; but often coming
out with frustration as they think
these are maps to nowhere.

Readers then rage at the incomprehen-
sibility of it all, a hopeless thought spree.
Why even split that word above?  That
is simply incomprehensible, something
that is everywhere here.

Poets then counsel patience. They tell
the readers that, if you make a church,
you must also make a steeple.
There really are answers.
But if you go to the poet's theater,
you must supply the dancers.

## THE POET'S SONG

The soul's waters flow from a hidden spring
where a nameless darkness hides from light.
The poet finds this place and returns to sing.

He finds that which wants to silently cling
and wait to release its grip till time is right.
The soul's waters flow from a hidden spring.

The poet takes his lute, softly plays a heartstring,
plays a song that sings, permeating twilight.
The poet finds this place and returns to sing.

The music of the spheres moves darkness to ring,
while the poet's strokes cause the unknown to ignite.
The soul's waters flow from a hidden spring.

The dross burns away, starlight shines on everything.
Fire brings a passing of darkness, farewell to night.
The poet finds this place and returns to sing.

At last truth into the open comes, bringing
its life before us, but now in a bright light.
The soul's waters flow from a hidden spring.
The poet finds this place and returns to sing.

# THE NEIGHBORHOOD

Most of us live in a neighborhood or once did, some kind of
neighborhood. Maybe a small town, maybe a section of a city.
Some live in the country where the nearest neighbors are
deer and rabbits, but I'm not talking about them, just the townies
or the city folk because that is what I know.

## WHAT IS THIS PLACE?

Massive, gray and rising,
full of unseeing eyes;
far above the hard path,
with gutters.

Hot or cold, too much,
too soon, too fast;
with broken pieces
down below.

And in between is the
colored invisible;
but not so hued as to
cancel dread.

A bit melodramatic,
great theater.

Looking again, seeing now
the cozy way, surrounded
by comforting walls,
reflecting light,
hot
cold
fast
abstract shapes in
concrete images
with colorful air
filled with sound.

Still melodramatic,
still great theater,
still the city.
Still

That was exhilarating, but let's go somewhere smaller and quieter.
And let's go at the most peaceful time of all, Sunday morning.

## SUNDAY MORNING SPEED

Cars parked,
one after another,
in a neighborhood.

These are different
from cars parked:
  in a mall
   or at the opera
    or in a field
     for the company picnic.

These cars are parked,
one after another,
in a neighborhood.

# THE MODEL RAILROAD

See that building
with red brick, low roof;
they sold Sunday best.
The yellow one:  a butcher, a green-grocer.

There is the railroad station
where my aunt went
to New York (via Scranton).
Mom and Dad and me waved good-bye.

And over there are houses
where coal miners lived,
next to the tracks, once
but not now, all gone.

I would like to visit
my aunt in Stone City,
but I don't know where,
or which stone.

# THE MAILBOX

The corner is the place
where two streets quietly join,
no matter if sun or clouds or dark,
or house or store or park
speak or snub the mailbox,
which alone just wants to be.

The mailbox has no desire to be
that which marks the place.
The place is on its own, mailbox
or no mailbox, the box refusing to join
the house or store or park
in either bright sun or inky dark.

Now someone comes in the dark
holding what seems to be
an envelope with stamp to park.
They lift the lid and place
their silent words inside to join
the secret interior of the mailbox.

Letters hide here in the mailbox,
epistles gathering in quiet dark.
Outside the human throng will join
each other, just wanting to be
clanging, banging, in their usual place,
while their papered words silently park.

At long last comes the mailman who park
salong side of the curb, by the mailbox,
which silently waits for the mailman to place
his key in the slot, and open to the dark
region, like reaching in a tomb to be
the one who removes the trinkets, to join

the survivors who walk, who join
others near house or store or park,
to become the forgetting, those that be
unaware of coming to this mailbox,
which now is gone to them as if in the dark,
even as this corner is now a lost place.

In the place above, "salong" seems to join
some dark idea that eludes me, as I park
and, oh where can that mailbox be?

# THE LOCAL NEIGHBORHOOD MUSEUM

At the museum, I saw
a billion year old artifact
from Europe.

The curator explained
that it was brought here
by Europe itself,
when it crossed and obliterated
a primeval sea

and collided
with North America.

It was left here,
like ancient luggage,
no longer needed
for the return trip, when Europe
went home

and the sea
returned.

And finally the sea moved over
and left
Virginia.

The museum is
just outside my front door
and down the steps
along the sidewalk.

The curator is
my son, the geologist,
who, around here,
is simply, my son.

And the artifact is
quartz, child of
sandstone, and pressure,
and time.

What we call

  a rock.


  As we are leaving the neighborhood, we are passing one of my
favorite places.  Let's go inside and browse for a while.

# USED BOOK STORE

Push open the door and hear the little bell tinkle

The nose knows first as it meets old book sweat

    a product of all those words all those years working
    filling minds with notions, thoughts, dreams, feelings

Where are those minds now and are their little bells tinkling

    and if they are are they all the wiser, the happier, fulfilled
    with what they were filled with

    or are they gone somewhere utterly unknown to us?

No matter, the old books are still here
  and they are still filled with their old words

  words ready to sweat again for a new reader
    for whom the words are not old
    or maybe they are, just old friends

Remember also life on the page; words live there,
  but words do not share

  they may guide, they may lead, they may enlighten, but
    words do not share

  they are guardians of thought, but a thought cannot be shared
    a thought can only be thought

So here in the Used Book Store wander the aisles seeking until
a book, covered with sweat but still strong speaks
with silent sounds, but soundings none the less

and we respond, putting our hand which is then
clasped by the cover to join our curious mind

Opening the book in the aisle of the Used Book Store

we see those words that guide, that lead, that enlighten
but they share nothing

we must encounter them, see them, caress them,
and take what we can, what we must

What then happens to the used book in the Used Book Store?

it may come with us to the clerk and become
a transaction

or it may stay on the shelf and resume its vigil
but either way the words have sweat again

What then happens to us who encountered the used book
in the Used Book Store?

We know the words do not share, do not care
but are still there even when we are long gone

But where ever we have gone, have we taken
what we ought?

# LAMENTATION

Sometimes, poetry deals with sadness.
Tears will flow but take heart:
Sooner or later, hope will return.
And though I do not wish to presume,
So Will Heaven

# LAMENTATION

Singing songs of woe,
Tearing the garments,
Wiping away tears.

Lamentation

Comes to all at times,
Or in strange places,
In odd or sad ways.

Lamentation

So abstract, unreal,
Exactly the way
We want it to be.

Lamentation

With sad songs,
With torn cloth,
With real tears,

     Is not what we want lamentation to be,
     But if it were not lamentation,
     Would we lament or merely fake?

Lamentation

That which makes us whole,
Which helps through our woe,
Clouds which hide the sun

Which is still there

# EZZARD CHARLES IS DYING

I read in the paper
    on a Monday morning
    that Ezzard Charles is dying.

It was a long time ago,
    1949 to be exact,
    that Ezzard Charles became the champ.

How could this be?
Heavyweight kings were named either
    Joe Louis or
    Jersey Joe Walcott.

It was the first time that my world
was shattered by a new name;
something different.
It would not be the last.

I was eleven and my grandfather was old.
My father was the big man
and I was a little boy.
And Ezzard Charles was the champ.

My grandfather liked the fights
and I liked my grandfather
so I liked the fights.
But Ezzard Charles?  The champ?

My father knew all.
All the names of the ballplayers and boxers.
He knew if they were any good.  (He was
  a boxer himself, you know.)
But he never told me about Ezzard Charles.

Not many years passed,
and Ezzard Charles was beaten,
and disappeared from sight.
But the world was no longer the same.

Again, not many years passed, and
my grandfather was beaten,
and disappeared from sight.
And the world was no longer the same.
Ezzard Charles changed it all,
or was he merely the sign?
And many, many years have passed
and the world has never been the same.

My son is eleven and my father is old.
I am now the big man
and the little boy is gone.
And I don't even know the champ.

I read in the paper
   on a Monday morning
   that Ezzard Charles is dying.

Ezzard Charles is dying,
   and we are dying with him.

# THEATER OF THE ABSURD

Tuesday my mother died. Yes. On Tuesday.
Maybe Monday. Then it could be Thursday.
What difference does a day make? What makes
a day besides a sound saying a rising and a setting?

Don't expect a heart is breaking from me
and I don't expect sympathy from thee
other than to see you standing there with
a confused silent face and hand toward mine.

Don't expect a confessional outburst
about my grief as if I was the first
to walk in this path with personal pain,
not sought or wanted but heavily there.

Don't expect a stunning revelation
about my encounter with divine elucidation
since God has chosen to sit in silence.
If I had any sense, I would join Him.

Instead, I look out at a stage where a play
unfolds to my eyes only, a show this day
from the mind's arena with a special
production of the Theater of the Absurd.

In this drama, played inside a rounded
white room, a tiny entrance, and surrounded
with players who have limited access,
there are as I look, only villains.

There is anger and pathos and just lost.
A spring day with a sudden storm and frost.
Do I keep looking and if so for what?
I want to go home but I don't know where.

I need to tell my self the curtain will fall.
Soon there will be a curtain call,
and then the theater will be dark.
Maybe then I can contemplate in silence.

Yes.   All of us will get hit by a bus.
 Lord have mercy on us.

This was written for my cousin Leo, a merchant seaman and a World War II veteran of the Merchant Marine.

RETURN TO HOME PORT, SAILOR

The land-locked lakes are freezing
water turning to ice.
The ships have sailed while believing
time comes and goes.

The others once were coming
to pay the price
and having spent their all,
putting to sea in plainclothes.

You stood on shore waving
once again to thrice,
then turned to begin returning,
with a pause to recompose.

Oh sailor, you worked the shore
as you did the sea,
as cargo was loaded and carried
you to others with bonhomie.

But as once your time had come
your time was now time to go.
You have paid the price, spent your all,
packed only your plainclothes,

waiting for the ice to melt

knowing that Love melts ice

# DANCING ROUND THE TOMBSTONES

In America, comes a time when summer sun
smiles on the tombstones, drying tears
and leaving salt behind.

The graveyard of the calendar where winter
fled, with spring well on the way to renewal
of creation.

With blood for fertilizer, fear and pain
and suffering sowing seeds in soil
ready for the rain.

So it says on stones, engraved with names
and dates, of birth, of death, of coming,
of going.

So we decorate the stones, we remember—
Decoration Day— when we can no longer
find them— Memorial Day.

So why the shore,
why the mountains,
why the smiles and celebrations
at backyard grills?

The salt: the salt for seasoning,
the salt for savor,
the salt for preserving
for those to come.

For what value death
If it serves not life?

# LEAVE TAKING

## AUTOBIOGRAPHY OR NOT AUTOBIOGRAPHY? THAT IS A QUESTION HERE IS AN ANSWER

We have come to the end of this book. Before we read the final poem, I would like to discuss a question that people often ask of poets: Is your stuff autobiographical?

The answer, an answer that all poets would probably give you, although I do not like to speak for others, is unequivocally YES and NO.

My dictionary, "The Random House College Dictionary——Revised Edition Deluxe", copyright 1975 defines "autobiographical" in part as "dealing with one's own experience". The definition of "autobiography"is "an account of a person's life written by himself."

Everything a person writes deals with his own experience. What he says has to have come from his mind. What else could be the source? So everything anyone says or writes, whether or not they are poets, comes from their own mind. It is not necessarily original. Singing the "Star Spangled Banner" from memory for instance is singing words that the singer did not write and is not now reading but is remembering.

An example of a poem in this book that is from my mind but not my experience is "Skiing In The Alps." My middle daughter Angela was the one who skied in the Alps. She told me what it was like and I wrote it down. She corrected or approved it where necessary and voila, there was the poem. And I have never in my life been in Europe or on skis.

Some things that poets write about come from their own experience but are not accounts of their own life. In this way they are not autobiographical. In my poem "The Local Neighborhood Museum", the geologist is my oldest son Christopher, who is a geologist in real life. And my oldest daughter Mary loves this poem and insisted that I put it in this book. The science is accurate also, but I put everything together in my own way.

"Bad Poem" was written when my youngest daughter Patricia got her first dog for her family. And I had my youngest son Joseph, an auto mechanic who can make engines hum like a poet makes words sing, in mind when I wrote "Sunday Morning Speed".

But with all this said, sometimes the poems are actually autobiographical, but each in a different way. "Dark and Quiet and Breathless" which follows immediately is a step by step account of my inner life. "Ezzard Charles Is Dying" is written out of my own life history. And the poem that closes the book——"The Rabbi's Piano"——is from the same place.

My final words: I enjoyed spending this time with you.

We will end quietly, although
I wonder if you would have wanted the piano.

DARK AND QUIET AND BREATHLESS
(while looking at Degas' "Before the Ballet" )


Picture a long wide room,
dark warmly cool carpets and colors on the wall, contrasting
with six ballerinas, moving, stretching, slowly,
one floor to ceiling curtained window, allowing some light.

Four dancers along the far left wall, on one leg each, like
graceful herons in green tutus, with arms outstreched
creating triangles of several sizes, triangles found when
they dance on stage, leaving it up to you to look.

Three of the herons are in shadows, just like the show
to come, knowing and not knowing what to expect,
as every presentation of one to another is totally new;
while the fourth, near the window's light, glows with hope.

On room's other side, two dancers sit on a bench and stretch,
the one on the left raising a leg in toast to the eyes which
look straight at her golden slipper, the other ballerina
bending as if the floor held answers to questions not yet asked.

In between the two sets of dancers is the floor's dark rug,
dark and quiet, almost invisible like the stage outside,
for which we long, breathless.

# THE RABBI'S PIANO

It was a time when everyone
looked like U.S. Marines.
Short haircut.  Clean shaven.

Except the Rabbi.
Lived up the street.

An orthodox man
with a beard and skullcap.
Holydays, paid a quarter
and gave a piece of cake

to turn on lights
and fuel the stove.

Suddenly, the Rabbi was moving.
To Philadelphia.

The Rabbi,
who chanted the prayers
of High Holydays,
and regular Saturdays,

(heard through the open
windows of the
Synogogue)

was moving
to Philadelphia.

On the day before
the truck was loaded
and began its run,

the Rabbi called me in,
me, who had
turned on his lights,
and fueled his fire,

and eaten his cake,


but never, ever,
lighted
the Synogogue,

me! and asked me
if I wanted The Piano.

Yes!!!

And it was mine!!!

Then the Rabbi was gone,
he had moved
far away.


It was a time when
I was young
and did not know.

And my parents
repainted it.

A light biege
rather than
the deep black.
Holydays. Paid nothing

to learn its beauty
and warm my soul.

Time passed and then
I was moving south,
farther than Philadelphia.

I,
who heard the chanted prayers,
through the open windows,
and received the piano,
and paid nothing,
was moving to Virginia.

On the day that I left,
I did not think of the piano,
or the Rabbi.


I left.

The Rabbi was gone,
and he was still
far away.




The years pass
to a time when I love
the beauty of the sound
of the music always playing.

Also a time when I wish
I had paid to learn
its deeper mysteries.

And I
was asked!!!

Me, who never
was asked
to lighten
the Synogogue,
was asked!!!

To a child, bright with youth,
from an aging man;
rich mahagony.
Holydays.


Today, my parents
are gone, and
I can no longer
keep the piano.

Someone must
want it; maybe
even someone
innocent.



Since it must go,
only to lovers.
All I ask
is to try to see
its beauty.

How do you know
the lovers?

Must they first
be loved?

The Rabbi is not gone,
and He is
never far away.